**W9-ARF-452**

# BLACK BEARS

*by Timothy M. Daly*

**Children's Press®**

An Imprint of Scholastic Inc.
New York  Toronto  London  Auckland  Sydney
Mexico City  New Delhi  Hong Kong
Danbury, Connecticut

Content Consultant
Dr. Stephen S. Ditchkoff
Professor of Wildlife Sciences
Auburn University
Auburn, Alabama

Photographs © 2013: age fotostock: cover (Alaska Stock), 12
(Kitchin & Hurst), 1, 2 foreground, 4, 5 background, 28, 46 (Michael
Jones); Alamy Images/Stock Connection Blue: 19; Bob Italiano:
44 foreground, 45 foreground; Dreamstime: 2 background, 3, 44
background, 45 background (Adrian Gabriel), 32 (Outdoorsman);
Getty Images/Jacques Demarthon/AFP: 31; iStockphoto: 5 top, 20
(Images in the Wild), 40 (Philip Casey); Photo Researchers: 24 (Linda
Freshwaters Arndt), 23 (Millard H. Sharp), 15 (Thomas & Pat Leeson);
Shutterstock, Inc.: 35 (ngarare), 5 bottom, 16 (ostill); Superstock, Inc.:
36 (Animals Animals), 8 (imagebroker.net), 11, 27 (Minden Pictures),
7, 39 (Thomas Kitchin & Vict/All Canada Photos).

Library of Congress Cataloging-in-Publication Data
Daly, Timothy M.
 Black bears/by Timothy M. Daly.
   p. cm.—(Nature's children)
 Includes bibliographical references and index.
 ISBN 978-0-531-26831-5 (lib. bdg.)
 ISBN 978-0-531-25476-9 (pbk.)
1. Black bear—Juvenile literature. I. Title.
 QL737.C27D29 2013
 599.78'5—dc23                    2012012194

1 2 3 4 5 6 7 8 9 10 R 22 21 20 19 18 17 16 15 14 13

# Black Bears

| | |
|---|---|
| **Class** | Mammalia |
| **Order** | Carnivora |
| **Family** | Ursidae |
| **Genus** | *Ursus* |
| **Species** | *Ursus americanus* |
| **World distribution** | North America |
| **Habitats** | Large forests, as well as lowlands and wetlands, areas with ample vegetation for food and trees for protection; in northern areas, have been found in tundra too |
| **Distinctive physical characteristics** | Usually black coat, but also brown, gray, cinnamon, or white; usually cream-colored long snouts; males grow to be more than 6 feet (1.8 meters) long and weigh up to 600 pounds (272 kilograms); females usually much smaller; powerful claws to hunt prey and defend against enemies; small eyes; rounded ears; short tail; shaggy hair |
| **Habits** | Typically active right before sunrise and in late evening; nap during day; tend to live and forage alone, except for mothers and cubs; spend warmer months roaming wide areas for food; often hibernate during winter months |
| **Diet** | Mainly eat insects, grasses, berries, and roots; sometimes eat fish and meat; carrion and garbage left out by humans |

# Contents

# CHAPTER 1

# The Bear Facts

On a quiet morning in the northwestern United States, sun shines through the treetops and down to the thick tangle of bushes covering the forest floor. In the distance, the sounds of cracking branches and rustling leaves begin to fill the air. Soon, an enormous black bear steps out from behind a large bush, sniffing the air as it walks. It pauses for a moment, smelling a tasty snack nearby. Calmly, the bear lumbers toward a bush covered in plump, red berries and begins to eat.

Despite their name, black bears are not always black. Some are shades of tan and brown, while others are gray or white. Some black bears have white markings on their chests, and most have cream-colored **muzzles**. With their incredible size and strength, these bears can be ferocious fighters. However, they are usually very peaceful animals. They prefer to run away or hide when they notice enemies approaching.

*Despite their fearsome appearance, black bears mostly eat plants and do not like to fight other animals.*

# Across the Continent

Black bears are found throughout many parts of North America, as far north as Alaska and as far south as northern Mexico. They live in 32 U.S. states, five Mexican states, and all but one of Canada's provinces. Experts believe that the total population of black bears is somewhere between 400,000 and 950,000.

Most black bears live in forest **habitats**. They are found throughout the Rocky Mountains in the western United States and Canada and throughout the Appalachian Mountains in the east. Many black bears also live in wetlands, such as those found in the southeastern United States.

Different colored bears are more common in certain areas than in others. For example, you are most likely to see a black bear that is actually brown in the western United States and Canada. Almost all white-colored black bears live on one island in British Columbia, Canada. The different fur colors help the bears blend in with their surroundings.

*Black bears with white fur are sometimes called spirit bears.*

# CHAPTER 2

# Kings of the Forest

Black bears are among the largest mammals found in North America. They grow to be about 6 feet (1.8 meters) long and 3 feet (0.9 m) high, and they can weigh up to 600 pounds (272 kilograms). Because they are so large and strong, adult black bears have almost no natural predators. The only natural threats they face are other bears.

When running, healthy bears can reach speeds of up to 30 miles per hour (48.3 kilometers per hour) in short bursts. They are also strong swimmers.

Black bears are known for their remarkable climbing ability. They wrap their legs around a tree as if they are hugging it and climb up to find food or hide from humans.

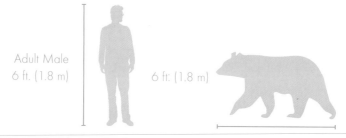

Adult Male
6 ft. (1.8 m)

6 ft. (1.8 m)

*Young black bears climb trees much more often than adults do.*

# A Varied Diet

Like humans, black bears are omnivorous. This means that their diet consists of both plants and meat. It is not an equal balance between the two, though. About three-quarters of an average black bear's diet is made up of plants. Black bears eat berries and other fruits, as well as nuts, seeds from pinecones, roots, and grasses. The bear's long tongue and flexible lips help it gather large amounts of these tiny foods.

Bears have considerable hunting skills. They kill and eat a wide variety of animals both large and small. They use their muscular legs and sharp claws to take down prey ranging from small forest mammals to young moose and deer. They also gather ants and other insects, eat honey from bees' nests, and snatch fish from the water.

Bears are opportunistic feeders. This means they will often eat any kind of food they can find, even if it is unfamiliar. Some bears even eat carrion or trash that humans have thrown away.

*Berries are a tasty treat for black bears.*

# Sights and Sounds

Black bears have excellent senses. They use them mainly to find food and avoid contact with other bears and humans. Though they have very small eyes, scientists believe that black bears can see about as well as humans can. Unlike many animals, they have the ability to see in color. This helps them spot the bright fruits that make up much of their diet. They are good at seeing moving objects and things that are close by, but they seem to have trouble seeing things that are far away.

Though it is impossible to tell exactly how well black bears can hear, scientists believe that they have much better hearing than humans do. Because they can't see very far, hearing allows them to notice danger from far away. It also enables them to notice threats approaching from behind.

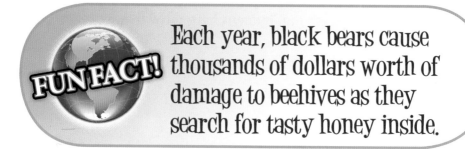

**FUN FACT!** Each year, black bears cause thousands of dollars worth of damage to beehives as they search for tasty honey inside.

*For animals with such large faces, black bears have very small eyes.*

# A Significant Sense

A bear's sense of smell is one of its most powerful and useful tools. Almost no other animal can compete with a bear when it comes to sniffing odors in the air. Even a bloodhound, a type of dog bred for its sense of smell, has only one-seventh the smelling ability a bear has. Bears use this incredible sense to find food, avoid enemies, and identify one another. Sitting up on their rear legs, black bears sniff the air to survey their surroundings. They have been known to smell prey from as far away as 40 miles (64.4 km), and they have noticed human scents more than 14 hours after people were last in the area.

Bears also use their sense of smell to communicate with one another. As they move around, they urinate and rub their bodies against plants. Other bears passing through pick up these scents and learn important information, such as whether the scent comes from a male or female or which direction the bear is moving in.

*Black bears can learn a great deal about their surroundings by simply sniffing at the air.*

# Warmth in Winter

Most black bears live in areas where it can get very cold during winter. They begin preparing for the harsh winter weather in late summer and fall by eating large amounts of food to increase their body fat. As the cold weather begins to set in, they move into their **dens**, where they will remain until spring. Most black bears use caves or **burrows** as their dens, but they have also been known to spend the winter in large piles of brush or inside hollowed-out trees.

Inside their dens, black bears enter a deep sleep that can last for months. During this time, they do not eat, drink, urinate, or defecate. They breathe less air and their heart rate slows. Their bodies get nutrients by burning the excess body fat that the bears built up before winter, and their heavy fur protects them from the cold.

**FUN FACT!** Between 1900 and 2011, just 63 people were killed by black bears.

*Some bears make their dens in holes dug out of the soil.*

# Lone Rangers

Black bears are mostly solitary. Each bear lives within a **home range**, which covers anywhere from 15 to 80 square miles (39 to 207 sq km). Home ranges are smaller in areas where there is more food. They are larger in places where the bear has to travel farther to get enough to eat. Black bears have excellent memories and navigation skills. This allows them to travel throughout huge areas without getting lost.

Black bears mark their home ranges by scratching marks on trees and urinating on the ground to leave their scent behind. Black bears are not territorial, though, which means they do not usually drive other bears from their home ranges. If there is a confrontation, however, black bears do something called jawing. During this display, the bears sit on their back legs, open their mouths, and softly growl at each other. The weaker bear usually backs away.

*Scratch marks can show bears when they have wandered into another bear's home range.*

# A Day on the Home Range

Black bears are most active in the hours around dawn and dusk. An average bear begins its day about a half hour before the sun comes up. The bear searches for food as it gets light outside, taking advantage of the cool morning weather. Black bears have big appetites, but the amount of time they spend **foraging** for food depends on the time of year and the weather. During a **drought**, when healthy plants might be scarce, a bear might have to travel great distances every day to find enough food. In spring, when food is plentiful and the bear does not have to worry about putting on weight for the coming winter, it does not need to spend as much time foraging.

Black bears often take one or two naps during the day. When it is warm outside, they tend to rest in the shade to stay cool during the hot midday hours. Most black bears bed down for the night between one and two hours after the sun goes down. However, some stay up late into the night to avoid running into humans as they search for food.

*Bears nap often during the middle part of the day.*

# Mating Season

One of the only times adult black bears spend time together is when they mate. The typical mating season for the black bear lasts for around two to three weeks each year. In warmer climates, it takes place as early as the first weeks of May. In colder areas, it might not occur until August.

Male black bears, also known as boars, often fight each other over the right to mate with a certain female, or sow. Soon after mating, the male leaves the female and returns to his solitary life. A female black bear might mate with several males over the course of one mating season. This means that cubs in the same litter sometimes have different fathers.

After mating season is over, the female begins eating and preparing for hibernation. About seven months after mating, she is ready to give birth. In most climates, this means she must wake from hibernation when her cubs are ready to be born.

*Male bears can become violent when competing for females during mating season.*

# Caring for Cubs

A mother bear gives birth to her litter in her den. A litter usually contains two or three cubs, but black bears have been known to have as many as six cubs at a time. Mothers giving birth for the first time usually have only one cub.

The cubs are born blind and helpless. Weighing only 7 to 16 ounces (200 to 450 grams), they are very tiny compared to their parents. Their fur is so thin that they appear naked. They stay close to their mother, warming themselves in her thick fur and nursing on the milk she provides them as food. After giving birth, the mother spends the rest of the winter in the den, taking care of her new cubs.

**FUN FACT!** A newborn black bear cub is about as long as a pencil.

*Newborn bear cubs need a lot of attention from their mother.*

# A Close Relationship

Black bear cubs are strong enough to walk and move around on their own when they are around five weeks old. Spring begins soon after this. The mother bear leaves the den with her litter for the first time, exposing the young cubs to many new dangers. Predators, such as wolves and other bears, hunt and kill bear cubs. As a result, black bear mothers stay close to their cubs and protect them fiercely. Sometimes the mother must leave her cubs alone and find food. She hides the cubs in tall grass or a hollow tree to help keep them safe from harm. The cubs howl to call her if they are distressed.

The mother bear continues nursing her cubs until they are around eight months old. Then she teaches them how to find food on their own. The cubs stay with their mother until the following spring. Then it is time for them to go off on their own so their mother can mate again and have a new litter of cubs.

*Mother bears teach their cubs the skills they need to survive.*

# CHAPTER 4

# Bears of All Kinds

Bears have been around for millions of years. Experts believe that the earliest bear species first appeared sometime between 55 million and 38 million years ago. Though they are **extinct** today, the ancient bear species are the **ancestors** of today's bears. Modern bear species first appeared about five million years ago.

Scientists have learned about these ancient bears by studying **fossils**. They use special methods to discover how old certain fossils are. This tells them roughly when the bears lived. They can also use the fossils to determine the ancient bears' sizes and habits. One species, the giant short-faced bear, was the largest that ever lived. These bears were around 11 feet (3.4 m) long and weighed around 2,000 pounds (907 kg). That is about twice as big as an adult male black bear!

*Many ancient bear species were gigantic compared to today's bears.*

# Nearby Relatives

In addition to the black bear, North America is also home to two other bear species. The brown bear is a large, bulky bear with a round face. These huge bears can weigh as much as 900 pounds (408 kg). In North America, they live in the northwestern United States, Alaska, and Canada. They can also be found in parts of Europe and Asia. Brown bears living in North America are often called grizzly bears.

Polar bears are slightly larger than brown bears, making them the largest bear species on Earth. On average, adult male polar bears weigh between 900 and 1,500 pounds (408 and 680 kg) and grow to lengths of about 8 feet (2.4 m). These huge bears are found only in the Arctic region, where the climate is extremely cold. Layers of fat beneath their skin and thick, heavy fur help keep them warm and dry in this icy environment. They mostly eat seals, whales, and fish. Their incredible swimming skills help them catch these aquatic animals.

*Polar bears live in cold, snowy climates.*

# Bears Around the World

Although they all live on the same continent, polar bears and brown bears are not the closest relatives of black bears. Instead, the black bear's closest relative is the Asiatic black bear. Found only in Asia, the Asiatic black bear is very similar to its North American relative. The biggest differences between them are that the Asiatic black bear is slightly smaller and has a moon-shaped patch of white fur on its chest. Because of the marking on its chest, it is also known as the moon bear.

There are four other bear species living throughout the world. South America is home to the spectacled bear, which gets its name from the light-colored fur around its eyes. Southeast Asia's sun bear is the smallest bear species. The shaggy, insect-eating sloth bear lives in the forests of India and Sri Lanka. Finally, the giant panda, famous for its distinctive black and white fur, lives in China and eats almost nothing but bamboo. Pandas are endangered.

*Asiatic black bears are known for their distinctive chest markings.*

# CHAPTER 5

# Living with Black Bears

Black bears and humans often share many of the same spaces. Whether it's a campground, a hiking trail, or even a town that is near a forest, there are plenty of places where humans and bears might cross paths. Black bears almost always prefer to avoid humans by hiding or running away. This doesn't mean they are harmless, though. A black bear can easily injure or kill a human.

People should never approach wild bears. If you ever encounter one, you should be sure to give it plenty of space. If the bear stops what it is doing to look at you, you are probably too close. If the bear starts moving toward you, do not run away. Instead, yell and make noise, or throw things at the bear. Most of the time, this will scare it away.

*Black bears can quickly tear apart campsites while searching for food.*

# Bad Behavior

Most black bear attacks are a result of human activities changing a bear's natural behavior. Because they are intelligent, opportunistic feeders, black bears can easily learn new ways to find food. If a bear learns that it can get food from humans, its habits can change drastically. It might lose its natural fear of people, so it would not run away when approached. It might also learn to beg for food or harm people in the attempt to steal from them. This is bad for people and bears alike. People can get hurt, and studies have shown that bears that subsist on human food tend to die much earlier than other bears. They are often hit by cars, and many get sick after accidentally eating food packaging.

Backpackers and campers are warned to keep their food and trash hidden to prevent bears from coming into their campsites. People who live near bears should make sure to keep their trash in bear-proof containers.

*Black bears are an increasingly common sight in suburban yards.*

# Thriving, Yet Threatened

While most bear species are threatened or endangered, black bears are thriving in most of the places where they live. There is very little danger that they will die out anytime soon. However, black bears are slowly disappearing in certain parts of North America. They are considered a threatened species in such states as Texas, Louisiana, Alabama, and Mississippi.

This is mostly because of human activities. Many bears are killed by accident, as a result of automobile collisions. Black bears must also contend with habitat loss as more and more humans expand towns, roads, and farms into the areas where bears live.

If humans follow the rules about dealing with black bears and work to help protect them from harm in areas where they are threatened, we will be able to share a safe and harmonious future with these incredible animals.

*Black bears that have lost their fear of humans often put themselves in dangerous situations.*

# Words to Know

ancestors (AN-ses-turz) — ancient animal species that are related to modern species

boars (BORZ) — adult male bears

burrows (BUR-ohz) — tunnels or holes in the ground made or used as a home by an animal

carrion (KAR-ee-uhn) — dead animal flesh

climates (KLYE-mits) — the weather typical of a place over a long period of time

cubs (KUBZ) — baby bears

dens (DENZ) — hidden areas where bears hibernate and give birth to cubs

drought (DROUT) — a long period without rain

endangered (en-DAYN-jurd) — at risk of becoming extinct, usually because of human activity

extinct (ik-STINGKT) — no longer found alive

foraging (FOR-ij-ing) — searching for food

fossils (FOSS-uhlz) — the hardened remains of prehistoric plants and animals

habitats (HAB-uh-tats) — the places where an animal or a plant is usually found

home range (HOME RAYNJ) — area of land in which an animal spends most of its time

litter (LIT-ur) — a number of baby animals that are born at the same time to the same mother

mammals (MAM-uhlz) — warm-blooded animals that have hair or fur and usually give birth to live young

mate (MAYT) — to join together to produce babies

muzzles (MUZ-uhlz) — doglike, extended noses and mouths on some animals

omnivorous (ahm-NIV-ur-uhs) — subsisting on a diet that contains both plants and meat

opportunistic (ah-pur-too-NIS-tik) — tending to take advantage of any available food source, even if it requires major dietary changes

predators (PREH-duh-turz) — animals that live by hunting other animals for food

prey (PRAY) — an animal that's hunted by another animal for food

sow (SOU) — adult female bear

threatened (THRET-uhnd) — at risk of becoming endangered

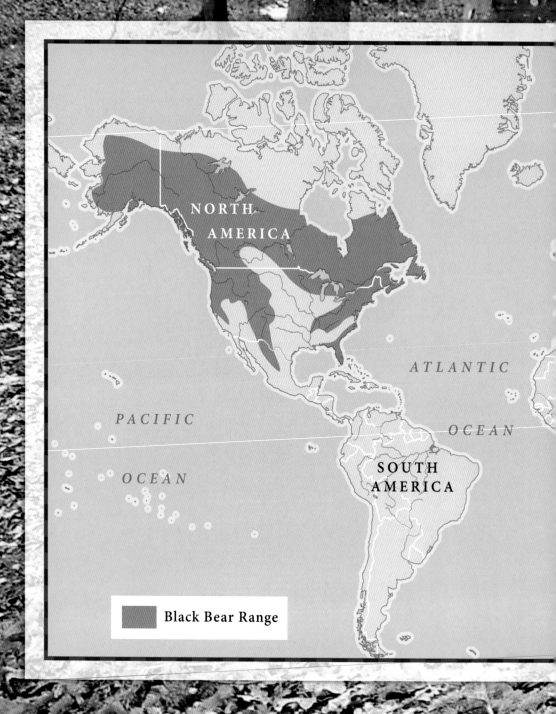

NORTH
AMERICA

ATLANTIC

PACIFIC

OCEAN

OCEAN

SOUTH
AMERICA

Black Bear Range

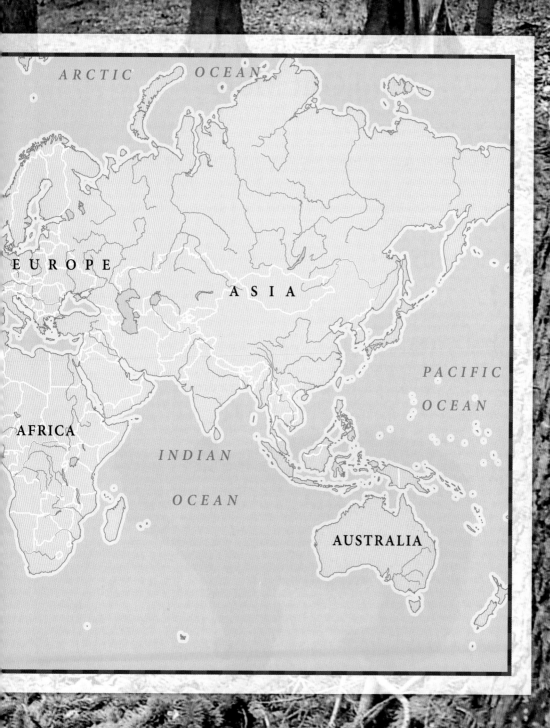

ARCTIC OCEAN

EUROPE

ASIA

PACIFIC

OCEAN

AFRICA

INDIAN

OCEAN

AUSTRALIA

# Find Out More

**Books**

Bailer, Darice. *Why Do Bears Hibernate?* New York: Marshall Cavendish Benchmark, 2009.

McAllister, Ian. T*he Salmon Bears: Giants of the Great Bear Rainforest.* Victoria, BC: Orca Book Publishers, 2010.

Sartore, Joel. *Face to Face with Grizzlies.* Washington, DC: National Geographic, 2007.

Visit this Scholastic Web site for more information on black bears:
**www.factsfornow.scholastic.com**
Enter the keywords **Black Bears**

# Index

# About the Author

Timothy M. Daly studied history at Western Connecticut State University, and has lived in New England his entire life. He enjoys spending as much time as possible outside, hiking and mountain biking. Having worked in children's book publishing for years, this is the first book he has written.